Stories from Mother

An Inspiring Book of True Stories &
Moral Poems for Children

Yashila Lobo

BookLeaf Publishing

India | USA | UK

To my spiritual mother, New Jerusalem, whose teachings have shaped many of these stories and without whom this book would not have been possible;

To my beloved mother, Shakila, whose love and guidance continue to inspire me from beyond.

Acknowledgement

First and foremost, I thank God Elohim. Without Their will, this book would never have been published. Their guidance and blessings have carried me throughout this journey.

I am deeply grateful to my dad, Andrew Lobo, for his unwavering support and guidance, which have been instrumental in bringing this book to life.

A special thanks to Siya Phogat, Priti Rajput, Angela D'Souza, Kalyani Jha, Lia Maria Fernandes, Olencio Zuzarte, Tiffany Percy Fernandes, Geetika, Reshami Jaiswal, Jonathan Jesus Viegas, Rakhee D'Souza, Vishakha Vikas Sinai Bhonsale, Andrew Lobo, Keegan Furtado, Dikshay Aldonkar, Ruth Josephine D James, and Lee-Ann Naomi Tavares. Each of you has inspired me in your own unique way and supported me on this journey.

Finally, thank you, dear reader, for choosing this book. I hope it brings you joy and inspiration!

Preface

"The heart of a mother is a deep abyss at the bottom of which you will always find forgiveness." – Honoré de Balzac

Hey there, little ones! Did you know the world could be a much better place if everyone thought with a mother's heart? You see, kids like you are quick to learn, but sometimes, what you see on TV or the internet don't always teach the best lessons. Don't worry, though—this book of fun, moral poems is here to help!

Most of these stories are inspired by the teachings of my spiritual mother, New Jerusalem, from the church I belong to, the World Mission Society Church of God. (If you're curious, you can learn more at www.watv.org.) These poems are designed to help you understand what's right and wrong and maybe even spark some ideas for making the world a kinder, happier place.

So, let's start thinking like a mother—with love, care, and a big heart. Who knows? Maybe one day, you'll change the world just by being YOU!

Siya's Joyful Discovery

In a faraway land called Sharesquare,
Lived a pretty little girl named Siya.
Innocent eyes, silky straight hair,
Cheerful, that's how you could describe her.

One fine sunny day,
"Ding dong," rang the doorbell.
Siya ran without delay,
Sped down the stairwell.

Siya opened the door in haste,
It was her neighbour Shaurya!
He was kind & angel- faced,
With a very charming aura.

Shaurya held out a tray:
"My mom made jalebis and sent some for you.
Could you keep the jalebis and give back the
tray?"
Siya's Mother said, "Come in, sit and I'll
return it to you.
Siya, follow me to the kitchen."
Filled with curiosity, Siya followed her
mother.
Mother held Siya's favourite chocolate, that
her uncle had given,
Like this chocolate, there was no other
It was only available abroad, not yet in India,
This chocolate was very precious to Siya.
But Mother wanted to give it to Shaurya.
"What? No! This is the last one!" cried Siya.
Mother said, "Siya, stop being stubborn.
You can't always have your way."
Siya was furious that her mother was so firm.
She ran after her mother to snatch the
chocolate away.
But alas! It was too late!
Mother had already given Shaurya the
chocolate!

When Shaurya took the first bite,
Mother saw Siya standing, filled with spite.
She expected Siya to scream with fury,
But what happened next was extraordinary...
Instead of anger, Siya felt joy.
She smiled at the little boy.
Shaurya was smiling and thanked them with
glee:
"I've never eaten this before! It's so tasty!"
Mother returned the tray and walked away,
But the joy in Siya's heart decided to stay.

"How did my anger turn into joy?" Siya asked
her mother.
"The joy of giving is magical..." explained her
mother.
"..Giving without expecting anything in
return can be a task,
But only then in the magical joy you'll bask.
'Giving love is more blessed than receiving it'
You'll always be happy if you follow it."

This incident deeply touched Siya's heart.
She felt this magic should be shared with everyone.
She thought and thought, and being very smart,
Siya came up with a plan that would be fun.

When Siya went to school, she ran to her teacher:
"Ma'am, for our class activity, I have a great thought!
I experienced the joy of giving, oh it was a wonder!
I also want my friends to feel this joy that can never be bought.
Could we visit the orphanage nearby?
We could give them gifts and also play some games,
But only if you comply."

The teacher approved Siya's suggestion,
And so began the preparation.
Each student was assigned a duty,
They worked with great unity.

Everyone was excited
To make the orphans happy.
And soon the day arrived,
Which they all anticipated.

Some prepared cakes and snacks,
Others made bookmarks with origami acts.
A skit, some songs, and goodie bags,
Games and decorations that were very pretty.
The children bonded with the orphans very
well.
They sang, danced, played, and ate together
It was indeed all so swell!
Siya smiled as she watched her classmates
altogether.

Every face was bright and beaming,
It was the magic of the joy of giving.
There were some classmates who often fought
with Siya,
But serving the orphans, they looked so dear.
Siya did not feel even a tinge of spite,
They all looked angelic; she forgot all the
fights.

Each face had a smile, nobody was sad
And soon it was time for them to go back.

What can we learn from the story above?
It's always better to give love.
If we lived daily as Siya and her friends did,
Wouldn't the world be splendid?
Remember: Give love without expectation,
And you'll receive joy and satisfaction!

Priti's Journey

Long ago, in the valley of bliss,
Lived a young woman named Priti.
She was an amazing artist
And also very pretty.

To admire her art,
People travelled from lands afar.
One day, Priti had a great idea—
Mount Dreamy wasn't far!
She could climb the mountain for the
amazing scenery;
It'd make a lovely painting for all to see.

Thus, she packed her art tools
And headed to Mount Dreamy.
But let me tell you,
The climb wasn't easy.
Yet once Priti reached the top,
She realised the climb was worth it.
And for a moment, Priti stopped
To marvel at nature's beauty.

The hazy pink sky blended with the blue sea;
Everything large looked rather tiny.
Colourful birds sang sweetly.
So touched by this was Priti
That she became emotional—
This view was utterly sensational.

So, Priti started painting.
Once she finished,
She heard someone panting.
Around looked Priti,
And she spotted an old lady,
Struggling to climb up.
So, Priti went and helped her up.
The old lady thanked her,
And with eyes filled with tears,

Said she wanted to climb Mount Dreamy for
many years.
And by God's grace,
She finally did it today.
They sat together to observe the beauty,
Speaking and laughing joyfully.
The old lady noticed the painting by Priti,
Admired it, and then said wisely:
"Your talent is wonderful, my dear,
But let's take a moment to admire
The greatest artist of all—God.
Look at the beauty around you,
The colours created by God—
Combinations of wonderful hues.
Though you may think you paint with your
own imagination,
What you paint is a copy of His original
creation."
Just before leaving, the old lady
Turned to Priti and said:
"Only to God belongs all glory.
Without God, we are nothing but dead"
Priti was humbled by this experience.

So at all her exhibitions, right at the entrance,
She always placed a huge board,
It read: "Glory be to the greatest artist: God."
Earlier, Priti had enjoyed the glory—
Until the day she had met the old lady.
But from that day onward,
Whenever people praised her work,
She would always say:
"Thank you for the kind words,
But I could only do this
With the help of the Almighty.
To Him belongs all glory."
Since Priti was so humble,
People spoke about her well.
Her audience grew and grew.
Priti had seen the old lady's words come true:
"When we give God all glory,
We will surely be blessed greatly!"

Angela & the Quilt of Love

In the little town named Shalom
Lived a woman, pretty wise and warm.
Her name was Angela,
Loved peace, not war.
She never fought with anyone,
And if she saw someone
Fighting with each other,
She would always stop the fight
Using all her might.

As Angela went to the market, one day bright
and fair,
She noticed people at the town square.

Usually, they lived in unity and peace,
But this day everything was amiss.
They were gathered, and they fought with one another,
Saying horrible things to each other.
When Angela saw this, her heart broke into pieces.
She thought to herself, "I need to stop this."

After much thought,
Angela came up with a plot.
She visited everyone herself,
And told them to gather at the town square.
With them they had to carry,
A piece of cloth with a special memory.

As agreed, all gathered,
Carrying pieces of cloth so colourful.
What would happen, they wondered,
As Angela appeared with some tools.

She handed out needles and thread.
"We shall all make a quilt together.." she said.
"...But as we make it, let us
Tell everyone why the cloth is so special to us.

Listening to each story,
We won't be fatigued.
Nobody should be bored—
It will be fun, rather than a chore."

Everyone agreed with great excitement.
As they listened to each memory,
Gave each other compliments,
Appreciated each and every story.
They stitched the quilt with great unity,
While getting to know one another.
Listening with great curiosity,
They soon understood
That everybody was good.
Unique and special was everyone,
And soon, the quilt was well done.
Once they heard every lore,
They wanted to fight no more.
No room for hate,
No more debates.
Only love filled their hearts for each other.

Everyone decided to place the quilt above,
The town square as a reminder of love.
The quilt looked brilliant,
Everyone was jubilant.
Each piece of cloth was special, beautiful in
its own way.
When sewn together, an awesome quilt was
made.
Likewise, while we are special in our own way,
When united, a loving clan is made.
Acceptance and love will overflow,
Joy and laughter spreads even more.
Each one plays an important part;
Only thing required is a loving heart.
And thus through the quilt,
The villagers learnt, for hatred, they weren't
built.
A truly beautiful mind
Belongs to the people who are kind.

And thus, peace in Shalom was restored.
Love, unity, and joy overflowed,
Thanks to Angela's plan, which taught them
to be kind.
She truly had the most beautiful mind.

So dear child, always remember:
Beauty is love, not hate.
With understanding and love for one another,
Let's not quarrel, but instead appreciate.
If you faithfully follow this,
Your life will surely be filled with bliss.

Pranav's Choice

Far far away in the land of Harmonyville
Lived a young boy named Pranav.
Love and joy did his heart feel,
A free spirit he did have.

He loved to visit the enchanted woods,
And on one bright sunny day,
Saw a magical clearing in the woods—
It appeared right in his way.

As Pranav looked with curiosity,
There before him grew two trees.
Both trees were magnificent;
One tree had leaves of diamonds,
The other had golden leaves.
Pranav had never seen such trees.

As Pranav was watching each tree,
A beautiful fairy greeted him.
Said her name was Kalyani,
And then she asked him,
"About the trees would you like to know
some more?
I am sure you've never seen them before!"

Pranav nodded excitedly,
And Kalyani continued with glee:
"Each diamond leaf grants a wish just for you,
While each golden leaf grants a wish for only
those around you
Think about this a little bit;
Then only one tree must you pick."
Pranav thought and thought.
The diamond leaf would make life easier;
It would help him a lot.

But then he also thought about everyone near
and dear—

Blessed by God, was he.
He needed to be helpful, not greedy.
Pranav with his heart of gold,
Stood up and to Kalyani told:
"I have finally made my decision,
I choose the golden tree with no hesitation."
Kalyani smiled and gifted him the tree,
Then she vanished, so did the diamond tree.
Pranav happily picked a few golden leaves.
He made the right choice, he firmly believes.
He ran home and placed them with care,
In a little tray, and then said a prayer:
For his best friend Ashwin, who was sick,
A leaf from the tray he did pick.
And off he went to visit Ashwin,
With faith that the leaf would cure him.
He ran as fast as he could,
To Ashwin's house in the neighbourhood.

Ashwin invited him in, weakly,
Pranav was hurt to see him in such a state.
He removed the leaf quickly,
And said with faith:
"Heal Ashwin, make him completely healthy."
The leaf turned to gold dust and entered
Ashwin's body.

The very next day everyone was surprised—
Ashwin was no longer pale now, rather
healthy and bright!
He was filled with so much energy;
People could not believe,
That the same Ashwin who couldn't move
yesterday,
Was playing football with his friends today!

When Pranav saw Ashwin healthy, he was
glad.
Ashwin needed the wish more than him.
With his choice he wasn't disappointed or
sad,
Choosing the gold leaf really helped Ashwin.

What Pranav didn't know,
That although
He chose the gold tree,
Something happened magically.
Whenever Pranav helped others,
His soul glowed brighter & brighter.
Thinking of others, his desires deprived,
God was proud of this little child.
Every time Pranav sacrificed something for
others,
God always rewarded him with something
better.

One night, Kalyani appeared in Pranav's
dream.
She looked glorious, surrounded by a beam.
"There are moments when
You choose to sacrifice yourself.
Though it may seem
Like you're losing everything,
With joy and blessings,
Your life will be filled."

Though just a dream,
Kalyani's message stayed with him.
Pranav continued to glow,
So, friends, what do we know?
The magic of loving others, giving in and
sacrificing
Always brings us much greater love and
blessings.

Lia's Tune of Understanding

In the tiny little village of Melodyhills
Lived a sparrow named Octavia.
Hearing her sing, everybody was thrilled—
A very talented sparrow was Octavia.
From dawn till dusk, she would sing and sing,
Joy filled the hearts of everyone listening.

However, one fine day,
A girl named Lia came to the village.
She was a travelling musician
Who won every competition,
And the hearts of people she did win,
Every time she played the violin.

Lia & her violin made a great pair,
And so she carried it everywhere.

Upon hearing about Lia,
Octavia had an idea.
She approached Lia
And boldly stated her idea:
"I, too, am a great musician
& challenge you to a competition.
In the end, we will see
Who performs more melodiously."
Octavia firmly did believe
That across the land and seven seas,
She produced the most beautiful sound;
Nothing better than her could ever be found.
She challenged Lia, as she was sure she'd win,
She believed herself mightier than Lia and her
violin.

The day of the competition arrived after all.
Everyone gathered in the village meeting hall.
Lia was to perform first.
She performed a tune no one ever heard.
The enchanting music filled the atmosphere,
The awestruck audience were moved to tears.

Then Octavia took the stage,
Proudly showing her vocal range.
With all her heart did she sing,
However she noticed something.
Though the audience didn't seem bored,
They enjoyed Lia's performance much more.
Though her performance was full of grace,
Disappointment was seen on everyone's face.
Compared to Lia her performance was
lacking,
She finished her song with a disheartened
feeling.
She had imagined that the audience would be
enthralled,
In reality, the audience was appalled.
Octavia realised that very moment,
That arrogance had clouded her judgement.

After the competition was over
Lia approached Octavia,
And said, "Your singing is so graceful,
But my violin also sounds beautiful.
We are amazing in our own way,
We mustn't compare ourselves in any way."

Octavia nodded humbly and agreed,
To the beauty in others she hadn't paid heed.
"Feeling sad when things didn't go my way,
Was a form of arrogance." she did say.

After this day, Octavia continued to sing,
While observing the beauty in everything.
We are all different creating a wonderful
harmony,
In our individuality lies true beauty.

Ollie's Wisdom

In the charming village of Diligence,
Lived some very hard working animals.
Working together they made their village
wonderful,
Each carried out their job with a mind very
joyful;
Building, cooking, cleaning,
And many other things.

Among the animals lived an owl named Ollie,
Who was known for his wisdom, not folly.
Ollie gave advice and helped everyone,
And thus as the village head he was chosen.

One bright sunny morning,
Ollie noticed a gathering,
They looked extremely unhappy.
Without hesitation they approached Ollie,
"Some animals aren't working as hard as us,"
they said,
This had made them very upset.
For instance, the rabbits complained that the
tortoises were slow,
And against many other animals they had
various woes.
Ollie listened to them patiently,
Then decided to tell a story:

"There was a busy village called Workerville,
And a lousy village called Grumpyville.
The animals in Workerville worked hard with
a smile,
While the people of Grumpyville only
grumbled all the time.
Workerville was taught that they each owned
the village,
With this mindset of a master, each would
manage
To do their job happily amidst laughter,

Never ever complaining about each other.
Grumpyville wasn't taught that they each
owned the village.
Of Workerville, they were an opposite image,
Without a master's mindset, they went
berserk;
Complaining and frustrated, everyone hated
to work."

Ollie asked, "Choose between Workville and
Grumpyville."
All the animals quite obviously chose
Workville.
Ollie said, "We too should work with a
master's mind,
Taking pride in our work, to each other being
kind.
Let us not complain about each other,
But rather let's encourage and help one
another.
If we do this, we will be happy like the
animals of Workville,
If we don't, we will be sad like the animals of
Grumpyville.
Complaining brings unhappiness,

Working with a master's mind brings joy &
happiness."

The animals of Diligence followed the advice
that they were given,
Together, they made Diligence a wonderful
haven.

Grumpy Learns Gratitude

Once upon a time in a lush valley,
Lived a giant named Grumpy.
He was strong and large,
The whole land shook when he marched.
Grumpy loved to complain, quite sadly,
About the weather, the food, and the
creatures of the valley.
Nothing was good enough for Grumpy,
He believed he deserved better, definitely.

One day as Grumpy was walking through the
valley,
He noticed some children playing with glee.
He stomped over to find out,
What were they so happy about?

Smiling, one of the children did say,
"It's because it's a beautiful day!"
Grumpy frowned and said rather quickly,
"But the sun is hot, the grass so prickly!"
The children ignored the grumbling and
continued to play,
They didn't want Grumpy's complaints to
ruin their day.

Over the weeks Grumpy complained and
complained,
Flowers were too colourful, water too plain.
Grumpy's complaints got too loud,
The valley was covered with a gloomy shroud.

One day while Grumpy was busy
complaining,
He met a wise monk who through the valley,
was passing.

"Did you ever think dear Grumpy,
That your complaints have made the valley
gloomy?"
Grumpy was shocked to hear the blame,
"But I deserve better!" he exclaimed.
The monk said, "Complaining can make you
blind,
To beauty & happiness of every kind.
Don't complain about what you don't have,
But be thankful for what you do have."

Grumpy realised that the valley was a place of
bliss,
He had been too busy complaining to notice.
From that day,
Grumpy changed his ways.
He stopped grumbling and began to see,
All the wonders of the once sad valley.

Thankful and humbled, he joined the
children's games,
And very soon he earned a new nickname.
Everyone decided to call him Happy,
For he was now kind and no longer grumpy.

Dear reader, arrogance comes from a mind
that grumbles,
It's always better to be thankful and humble!

Tiffany's Magic

Long ago in the land of Symphony,
Lived a beautiful girl named Tiffany.
Whenever she complimented anything,
Magical stuff would start happening.

One day Tiffany went to the town square,
She saw Mr. Fernandes tending to his garden
there.
His flowers were so beautiful,
That whoever looked at them became very
joyful.
Tiffany complimented, "Each flower seems to
be smiling at me!"
Hearing this, Mr. Fernandes glowed brightly.

The magic compliment began to show its
power,
Greener and vibrant turned every flower.

As Tiffany began to walk towards the ranch,
She saw Jason sketching a bird on a branch.
Tiffany complimented his work, smiling,
"Jason, you have a talent for drawing!"
Jason felt touched and he glowed more and
more,
Never had he received a true compliment
before.
As the magic of the compliment began to
work,
A gentle breeze carried his artwork,
Straight to the art teacher of Symphony,
Seeing his talent, he offered to train him for
free.

Magical things happened when Tiffany
praised someone genuinely,
Whenever she paid a compliment the town
sparkled brighter,
The people around her felt appreciated and
happier.

Tiffany never wanted anything in return,
The well-being of everyone was her only
concern.

One evening, everyone in Symphony,
Gathered together to thank Tiffany,
Each person complimented Tiffany.
They appreciated her kindness genuinely,
Each compliment did some magic unfold,
As though her kindness had been returned
tenfold.
She was enveloped by a glowy shimmer,
She felt warmth and joy within her.

Soon the village started a new tradition,
With Tiffany as its inspiration.
Every week at the town square,
The magic of compliments they would share,
In this way, the land of Symphony
Was always filled with bliss thanks to Tiffany.

Dear friend, compliment everyone, it doesn't
cost a penny,
It will surely fill you with love and joy
ultimately.

Geetika's Story of the Sea

In a faraway land,
Within a forest grand,
Lived Geetika the unicorn,
Of the forest, she was the first born.
Known for her wisdom and genuinity,
She often spent her time by the sea.

One fine day, as Geetika stood by the trees,
She saw magical creatures playing near the
sea.
Among them, was a mischievous pixie.
He was aptly named Rudy,

He loved pointing out other's faults.
He found joy in making others feel small.
Geetika approached & greeted them with a
voice so kind:
"Isn't the sea lovely? It washes our worries &
cleanses our minds."
Hearing Geeitka's kindness Rudy didn't know
what to say,
People always yelled at him and shooed him
away.
Geetika said, "Just as the sea purifies all that is
dirty,
Our minds can cleanse all negativity.
Pointing faults will create a whole mess,
Every situation should be dealt with kindness.
Our smiles will then be brighter,
And our hearts will be much lighter."

Rudy and friends agreed and decided to try
this,
Very soon their lives were filled with bliss.
Though they felt like pointing faults in one
another,
They became more understanding of each
other.

As Geetika strolled through the forest at
sunset,
She saw Rudy looking quite upset.
Geetika said, "Is everything okay Rudy?"
He said, "Being kind is a struggle, pointing
out faults is so easy."
Geetika nodded, "We all have faults, but just
like the sea,
Our kindness purifies it amazingly.
Rudy understood that covering others faults
made others happy,
While he himself felt light and joyful,
actually.

Rudy was soon a source of love & kindness,
He was no longer seen as a complaining rude
mess.
As he continued to cover the faults of others,
The sea of blessings in his heart grew deeper.

What do we learn from Geetika's wisdom?
Always choose kindness over criticism.
Everyone's fault we must cover,
And soon we will discover
That in our life, love and understanding will
flow freely,
As free as the sparkling, magical sea.

Reshami & the Grand Oak

In a village filled with serenity,
Lived a humble shepherdess named Reshami.
She was greatly respected by all,
For her gentle nature and her faith in God.
She believed that no matter how talented one maybe,
They should always walk the path of humility.

One morning, as Reshami was leading her sheep,
She came upon a magnificent tree.

It was grand and imposing,
With a haughty voice, it began to sing:
"I am the Grand Oak, look at me I'm so mighty,
I'm stronger and more beautiful than any other tree."
"This tree is so arrogant," thought Reshami.
She smiled and replied with humility,
"Grand oak you are a magnificent tree,
But do remember— you are created by the Almighty.
Though you may be sparkling with magnificence,
Always remember to be humble in His presence."

The Grand Oak shook and said aloud,
"I am greater than all, including God!"
Reshami sighed and walked away from the proud tree,
She knew the Grand Oak would learn a lesson, eventually.

As the seasons changed, a storm swept
through the terrain,
Along came strong winds and very heavy rain.
Grand Oak tried to stand tall,
But alas! It had a mighty fall.
The forces of nature humbled the Grand Oak,
To help him, rushed all the village folk.
Among the crowd, stood Reshami.
And she whispered humbly,
"Even the mightiest of all trees,
Must bow before the Almighty."
The villagers agreed and helped Reshami,
To replant the Grand Oak— an act of
kindness and humility.

From that day once again the Grand Oak
stood mighty,
But it had learned a valuable lesson of
humility.
It was no longer boastful and haughty,
But rather stood as a symbol of power of the
Almighty.

Through this story we can learn,
No matter how talented or how much you
earn,
God is the one blessing us all right from the
start,
Always follow God with a humble heart.

Johnny's Sacrifice

A long time ago, in a fantastical valley,
Lived a young boy named Johnny.
Known for his kind heart, he helped many,
He dreamed of filling everyone's hearts with
glee.

One day, as Johnny helped his friends with
their work,
A wise woman, Vienna, noticed how selfless
Johnny was.
Vienna was known throughout the valley,
For her connection to the forces of mystery.
Vienna said, "In order to become a vessel of
light,
You must be willing to sacrifice."

Johnny always wanted to be a source of light,
He asked her, "What do I need to sacrifice?"
She said, "It should be a prized possession,
Then the universe will know your hearts
condition.
The sacrifice will show the universe,
Your commitment to spreading goodness."

Johnny thought about the sacrifice harder
and harder,
He thought about a locket that belonged to
his father.
Johnny truly treasured it and wore it
everyday,
It contained a picture of his father who had
passed away.

With a heavy heart, Johnny made the
sacrifice,
He kissed it for the last time and threw it in
the sky.
Into a star, the locket transformed,
Johnny's appearance took a shimmering form.

Johnny smiled as he realised,
The sacrifice unlocked some new power deep
inside.

From that day, Johnny became a vessel of
light,
With everyone he shared this newfound light.
It was through his true selfless sacrifice,
That Johnny could brighten everyone's lives.

One day, as Johnny sat on the sand,
The locket star descended into his hands.
He smiled as he understood,
His sacrifice made him selfless and good.

Vienna appeared and said, "To become a
greater vessel in life,
We should always be willing to sacrifice."
Johnny nodded and agreed,
Holding on to extra possessions is only greed.
In your life, miracles will start,
When you give to others with all your heart.
Dear Reader, always keep in mind,
It's through selflessness that we truly shine.

Rakhee's Service

In a beautiful village, lived a woman named
Rakhee.
She always loved to serve others with dignity.

One morning Rakhee saw some children
playing,
They were having a wonderful time while
laughing and running.
Rakhee wanted to make their day even better,
She approached them amidst the chatter:
"How would you all like a picnic treat?" said
Rakhee,
The children agreed and danced joyfully.

Rakhee spent the morning,
Cooking and baking.
A cake, sandwiches, jelly,
Fruits, and chips— she packed lovingly.

"Here's your treat, friends!" said Rakhee,
The children rushed to her excitedly,
Looking at their happy faces, Rakhee herself
was filled with bliss.
Knowing that she made their day better,
through her act of service.

Rakhee sat down and began to think deeply,
She remembered many stories of the
Almighty.
"Though He is powerful and mighty,
He came to serve humanity.
Serving others always pleases the Almighty,
When we serve others humbly, blessings will
be plenty."

One day, the villagers decided to thank Rakhee,
For her service, love and humility,
Rakhee said, "When we serve others with love,
We reflect the saviour above.
Just as God came to serve us all,
We must also serve one and all.
It is surely in this way,
Abundant blessings will come our way."

The villagers agreed with Rakhee,
They decided to help each other cheerfully.
The village was an abode of love, kindness, and service,
The villagers were united without any malice.
They were making each other happy with acts of love,
Most importantly they pleased the one above.

What can we learn from the story of Rakhee?
Serving others is a sure way of receiving blessing.
Always serve others with joy and love,
And you'll surely please God above.

Andy's Gift of Hope

Once upon a time in a lush green valley,
Lived a happy little boy named Andy.
One evening, as he sat to draw,
He overheard news of war.

Soldiers marched through the streets,
People separated from their families.
Food soon became a scarcity,
People lived in uncertainty.

Andy's father was an officer known for
bravery,
Thus, he was called to serve immediately.
Before he left Andy said,
"It feels like this suffering will never end."

Though burdened by his own worries,
Father said to Andy very gently.
"War brings suffering for everyone
But remember, suffering won't go on and on,
Endure with faith, courage and kindness,
In Heaven, you'll be rewarded for your
goodness."

"What do you mean papa?" asked Andy, in
confusion quite curiously.
Showing both strength and kindness, Father
replied lovingly,
"In heaven, there is a place where there is no
war, no hunger, and no pain,
Those who endure life's hardships with
kindness, eternal joy they will gain.
Stay strong, help each other and always
believe,
To Something beautiful our trials will lead."
Andy listened to his father and obeyed him
courageously,
Though there was little to eat and nights were
filled with fear,
Andy always sincerely helped his mother and
many others.

One day, after he had finished studying,
Andy was surprised to see his favourite
pudding.
In these tough times it was a very rare treat,
Andy's eyes lit up, he could hardly wait to eat
it.
Just as he was about to take his first bite,
He noticed a weary soldier passing by.
"Excuse me.... "said the soldier weakly,
"Could you spare a bit of food for me?"

Andy looked at his pudding,
For this pudding he had been longing.
In these troubled times of war,
Should he give away what he had been
longing for?
But then Andy came to remember,
The wise teaching of his father.
He gave the soldier his bowl of pudding,
"Thank you," said the soldier, his voice
trembling.

The soldier ate and said, "Your kindness shows strength,
Andy, may your good heart always be blessed."

Andy realised that giving up for someone who needed it more,
Was the kind of strength his father had spoken of before.
Though his stomach was empty,
His heart was filled with glee.

Weeks passed and eventually the war was shut down,
Soon Andy's father returned safe and sound.
Andy's village was once again a safe haven,
Andy had learned a powerful lesson.
By enduring with faith and courage, being kind,
One can bring light to the darkest of times.
Those who endure with hope, joy, and love
Will be rewarded on earth as well as in Heaven above.

Vishaka's Change of Heart

Vishaka was a girl from a bustling town,
She was rude and always wore a frown.
Spoke roughly and pushed everyone away grumpily,
The townsfolk wondered why she was so unfriendly.

The truth is Vishaka hadn't always been this way,
She was kind and full of laughter everyday.
By carrying heavy bags, she helped the elderly,
And even fed stray animals daily.

However, over time,
People took advantage of her being kind,
They would say rude things behind her back,
Many jokes about her they would crack.
Although she tried to help them,
All they did was hurt her in the end.
She believed if she was rude first, she
wouldn't be in pain.
In this way, no one could ever hurt her again.

One day, the town was hit by a storm.
Rain poured down like a gushing waterfall.
Vishaka's house was in danger of being
flooded,
She struggled to keep the water out, she
didn't quit.
Cold, wet, and scared was she,
Never before had she felt so lonely.
Just when she thought she couldn't handle it
anymore,
A gentle knock came at her door.

Despite how rude Vishaka was,
Vikas came to help her without any qualms.
Along with him came Seema, his spouse
Using buckets they cleared water from the
house,
Kaniz joined them with some homemade
soup,
Meanwhile Pranav helped repair her roof.
They all worked together, laughing, and
encouraging each other.
Vishaka thought, "I have been so rude to
them, why do they even bother?"
Vikas said, "We know that some incidents
have left you forlorn
But we're here to show you that you're not
alone."
Hearing this Vishaka's eyes were filled with
tears,
She allowed herself to feel the kindness and
love around her,
Vishaka thanked them joyfully.
Soon the storm passed and there was serenity.

As Vishaka looked at those who helped her
through the storm,
She didn't want to be grumpy to them, but
warm.
Vishaka smiled and made a promise to the
one above,
That once again she would help others, laugh,
and love.
To those she had hurt, she began apologising,
Made every effort to be more patient and
understanding.

Dear child, some people may be rude,
But we don't know what has spoiled their
mood.
Though someone is rude to you,
Try to imagine their suffering too.
Be kind to everyone without exception,
And God will surely bless you for your
compassion!

Keegan's Lesson in Empathy

Keegan lived in a village next to a forest,
He was respectful, responsible and very
honest.
Friends and family he had aplenty,
To protect them he could even be a little
sneaky.

One day, while Keegan was playing with his
friends he heard a strange noise,
"What was that?" asked Viola with a
frightened voice,
They noticed the noise was coming from the
forest eerie,

Keegan said, "I'll go check it out, don't
worry!"
As he walked into the forest, the growl
sounded louder this time,
Keegan was worried about his sister Kay who
was playing nearby.
No matter what was lost,
Keegan decided to protect his sister at all
costs.

He followed the sound of the growl,
And came upon a large wolf sniffing around.
To get help, he wanted to go back,
But he couldn't waste time as the wolf could
attack.
He saw a fallen branch and a cluster of rocks
on his way,
Using this to make a noise, he scared the wolf
away.
Though the wolf looked like it would attack,
Keegan didn't rest,
The wolf hesitated, then went into the depths
of the forest.

Keegan protected his village & with relief he
did sigh,
However, he heard a soft whimpering nearby.
He discovered a small wolf trembling,
He realised the wolf was searching for her
baby, not hunting!
The pup looked at Keegan with frightened
eyes,
Keegan felt a pang of guilt as soon as he
realised.
To protect his own he was so busy,
He didn't realise he separated a mother from
her baby.

When he told his friends what had happened,
They called him brave and cheered.
However, Keegan felt uneasy,
He went home and told his mom the story.
His mom said, "Protecting your loved ones is
great my dear,
But sometimes when we act out of fear.
We can cause harm unknowingly,
Remember all creatures have their caring
families."

Keegan thought about this deeply,
And he lifted up the pup carefully.
And placed it where he had last seen the wolf
mother,
He waited patiently for an hour and another.
Soon the wolf mother came and sniffed her
baby with glee,
She picked it up and disappeared into the
forest joyfully.

From that day Keegan protected his loved
ones,
But made sure he wasn't hurting anyone.
Our bravery and honesty will definitely show,
When we are kind even to those we don't
know.

Through this story what have you been
learning?
Always balance bravery with empathy and
understanding!

Step by Step with Dikshay

Dikshay was a curious boy by nature,
He had a big dream of becoming an animator.
He imagined worlds where cats could talk,
objects could dance,
However, when he sat down to create, he felt
he did not stand a chance.
He would feel more overwhelmed with each
passing day,
The idea of becoming a great animator
seemed so far away.

One day, Dikshay went to his older brother,
He was kind, creative, and a great achiever.

Dikshay said, "I want to be an animator, but I don't think it's possible.
Reaching such a big dream seems so fantastical."
His brother smiled warmly and placed a hand on Dikshay's shoulder,
"Every big dream starts with small steps, my little brother.
If you try to leap straight to the end,
You'll only remain frustrated and scared.
Instead set some small tasks, work on mini goals,
These will help your dreams seem close."

"Mini goals? What do you mean?" said Dikshay, awestruck.
His brother said, "Break your big goal into smaller ones,
Focus on each step instead of going haywire,
Each step will get you closer to becoming an animator.
Though currently, this may seem berserk,
You've got to trust me, it actually works!"

Talking to his brother made Dikshay feel
encouraged and glad,
He wrote down his mini goals in a notepad.
Goal 1: Draw simple characters on my book.
Goal 2: Create a short, animated flipbook.
Goal 3: Watch tutorials on animation
software.
Goal 4: Make a 10-second animation and show
my family and those who care.

At a time Dikshay focused on one mini goal,
First he drew simple characters, quite
colourful.
His drawings were not perfect right away,
But they improved with each day.
After completing this, Dikshay worked on the
flipbook,
He decided to draw a small bird flying nook
to nook.
On his flipbook he worked day and night,
He finally flipped through it quickly and to
his delight,
The bird seemed to move, it was his first
animation!

He felt excited about the possibilities ahead,
there was no more confusion!

Next, he watched online tutorials, studying
all day in his chair,
He soon learnt to use animation software.
Now he could animate characters on his
computer screen,
This was what he had always dreamed.

Soon, Dikshay finished his ten second
animation,
Of a cat driving to the bus station.
Dikshay was overjoyed and he
Showed his animation to his family.

His parents and brother were amazed,
"This is fantastic, Dikshay! You've come so
far!" they exclaimed.
Dikshay realised that focusing on small steps
helped him progress more,
The big dream of becoming a great animator
didn't seem so distant anymore.

His brother smiled and said lovingly,
"A life without goals is like wandering
aimlessly,
By setting the smallest goals,
Step by step you'll find your way.
Your dream will be more attainable,
Fear and worry will go away."

From that day on, whenever Dikshay felt lost
and uneasy,
He sat and made mini goals to bring him
closer to his dream.

Dear friends, rushing to the end isn't the right
way,
Learn to enjoy every step along life's way.
A life with no goals is meaningless and empty,
Always set mini goals for yourself, you can do
whatever you please.
With small steps and clear direction, any
dream can be reached!

Josie's Bike Adventure

Joshua and his older sister Josie,
We're riding their bikes to the park when suddenly,
Josie's bike made a strange noise.
"What was that?" said Josie with a trembling voice,
She got down the bike and noticed that,
The tire had gone flat!
"We need to fix this!" groaned Josie,
Joshua said calmly, "Let's go to the bike repair shop, don't worry!"

They hurried over to the mechanic's shop at
the end of the street,
The mechanic was an old man with a frown;
he didn't look very sweet.
"What do you fools want?" he grumbled,
Feeling nervous but determined Josie
fumbled.
"My b..b.. bike has a flat tire, could you fix it
please?
The mechanic frowned, his face full of grease,
The mechanic groaned heavily.
He said, "You idiots should have ridden more
carefully!
What do you think, fools?
Should I leave all my work just for you?"

Josie felt anger bubbling up inside her.
"Why is he being so rude?" she whispered to
her brother,
But Joshua just smiled gently.
"We'll wait...," said Joshua to the mechanic
politely,
 "...Thank you for helping even though you're
busy."
Josie's cheeks flushed red.

Why was Joshua not angry, but calm instead?
Josie felt it wasn't fair.
She felt that Joshua didn't care,
Josie said, "Joshua, why aren't you saying
anything?
He's being mean when we have done
nothing!"
Joshua looked at Josie and smiled,
"Josie, it's always better to be kind.
Though someone is mean to you,
You never know what they're going through."
Josie crossed her arms, still angry.
She watched Joshua thank the mechanic for
helping them cheerfully,
The mechanic said he would take some time,
So Josie and Joshua visited a book store
nearby.

Josie couldn't stop thinking about what
Joshua had said.
She wondered how things might have been if
they had been rude instead.
The mechanic would get angrier and would
have sent them away.
The next repair shop was miles away!

Travelling there would be bothersome,
Being mean would have surely worsened the situation.
She was glad that Joshua's kindness kept things calm,
Being rude wouldn't have helped after all!

When they returned to the shop, they were surprised,
To see the mechanic greet them with a bright smile.
The mechanic said, "Hey kids! I had a really rough day,
It was wrong of me to take it out on you that way.
Thank you Joshua for being polite,
You two are an absolute delight!"

Josie's eyes widened in surprise.
She hadn't expected the mechanic to apologise.
The mechanic smiled and continued,
"I'm giving you a discount on the bike repair.
It's the least I can do."

As they left the shop, Josie smiled at her
brother.
She said, "You were right. Being kind is
always better."

Dear reader, always remember this:
Every situation can be dealt with love and
kindness.

Lee-Ann & Bruce

Once upon a time lived a young girl named
Lee-Ann,
She adopted various animals as part of her
clan.
She loved all the animals dearly,
But her favourite was Bruce, her puppy.
He was her protector, playmate and best
friend.
He followed Lee-Ann wherever she went.

One day, when Lee-Ann was ten,
Something very terrible happened.
Bruce was playing near the trees,
When a deadly cobra slithered under the
bushes.

Before anyone could react, the cobra struck
Bruce,
Lee-Ann was nearby gathering some fruits.
Hearing Bruce cry and yelp,
Lee-Ann dropped her fruits and rushed to
help.

Lee-Ann's heart broke as she watched her best
friend in pain,
She tried everything possible, but it was all in
vain.
She gently patted his head, crying
She whispered, "Please wait Bruce, Papa is
coming."
Bruce understood what Lee-ann said,
And when Papa arrived he lifted his head.
With all remaining energy, Bruce's tail gave
one last wag,
Never once did he show them he was sad.
Bruce let out a peaceful sigh,
And with that, for the last time he closed his
eyes.

Watching him die, Lee-Ann cried and cried,
But she also felt something deep inside.
Bruce had been a friend to her from his birth
to death,
He was loyal to her until his very last breath.
Lee-Ann realised that animals aren't objects
or mere playthings.
Just like humans, they have love, loyalty and
feelings.
Even when he was struggling, he stuck by her
side,
This amount of love may not even be found in
humankind.

From that day, Lee-Ann's mission was to care
for animals of every nature.
As she grew older, she started working at an
animal shelter,
Everyday she helped sick and injured animals,
remembering Bruce.
She treated them with love, knowing they
have feelings too.

One day, a little boy visited the shelter to adopt a pet.
"I don't think this stray can even care about me," said he, quite upset.
"Animals have hearts just like us..." said Lee-Ann smiling,
"...If you love him, he'll love you back more than you can imagine."
The boy smiled and decided to adopt the puppy,
Together they looked extremely happy.

Through her work at the shelter, Lee-Ann spread the notion,
That like people, animals too were God's creation.
They deserve all the love in the world.
In return, they will love you tenfold,
Even to the point of death.
So remember dear friends:
Animals should never be beaten or treated harsh,
They are faithful friends who love with all their hearts.

www.ingramcontent.com/pod-product-compliance
Lightning Source LLC
LaVergne TN
LVHW011043200726
843509LV00011B/1341